Craft Class

Stacey Osbeck

Copyright © 2019 Stacey Osbeck

This book is a work of fiction. Any references to historical events, real people, or real places are used fictitiously. Other names, characters, places, and events are products of the author's imagination and any resemblance to actual events or places or people, living or dead or undead, is entirely coincidental.

Author photo by Erika Osbeck

Published by Wildest Dreams

All rights reserved.

ISBN: 978-0-9600507-2-7

1

"I can't believe Dad got you a gift for my birthday *again*," Holly said flicking the high beams to make sure they were on. Heavy snowfall caked the headlights turning the road and fields dark, as dark as white can be at night.

"He doesn't mix them up every year," Grace said.

"But he remembers you on your birthday and you on my birthday."

"He's a sonofabitch, what else is new? You can have the scarf. I don't want it."

"I don't want it either."

"We both got Christmas gifts," Grace said, throwing her dark hair into a quick workout bun.

"I was born two days after Christmas. I was named after a Christmas plant. There's snow on the ground. Could these be clues?" Holly said. "Mom wouldn't have screwed them up. Remember she used to--"

"--Watch! Watch!"

The Buick fishtailed. The skidding, the

flipping, the landing upside down seemed to happen all at once. Glass beaded in a thousand directions. The older car deployed no airbags. Gravity pulled in the wrong direction. Seatbelts kept them strapped in and suspended. Their rears hovered mere inches from the seats.

"Are you ok?" Grace blurted out in a voice she didn't recognize.

Holly, still clutching the steering wheel, offered only confused blinking. The end of her sandy colored ponytail lightly touched the felt ceiling. With the buffer of glass gone, a sharp wind cut through their long sleeve tees. Grace's mind leapt to Grandma's advice from long ago: Don't dress for the car. Dress for the weather. They'd flung their coats and gloves and everything else in the backseat.

Grace twisted her shoulders struggling to reach the heavy jackets now flopped on the interior of the roof among the stray contents of their purses. Her fingertips barely brushed the closest shearling collar. She pushed one hand on the dash trying to gain a few inches. Pinching the fleece between her fore and middle finger was not nearly enough to get a good tug, no matter how hard she fought. Rather quickly her muscles took to shaking from the biting December winds.

"I can't reach the goddamn coats," Grace

said.

When Holly still didn't respond, Grace stopped stretching.

Without expression, Holly said, "I'm slipping." Her eyes rolled back into her head and her lids closed for the last time. Holly's grip loosened and her hands slid from the wheel, the left wrist hitting the roof liner with a thud. An instant before the other hand struck, Grace snatched hold of it.

With nothing else she could do for her, Grace brought her younger sister's hand to her mouth, blew warm air and whispered, "Someone will come. Don't let go." She continued with words of encouragement until of course the temperature and the elements took her as well.

2

Misty fluffiness enveloped their legs, dissipating at their waists. A bright cloud landscape swept before them as far as the eye could see. Off in the distance, they vaguely made out a man at a high podium. As they got closer a white wall with tall gates came into view. They stopped a few feet in front of him, with necks craned up, wordlessly waiting.

The man in white robes at the high podium thumbed through the pages of a monumental book, rest his gaze on Holly and said, "Welcome." The sisters looked to each other elated. He flipped to the next page and his demeanor changed. He took a long deep breath before addressing Grace, "Says as a child you played video games instead of saying your nightly prayers."

Grace listened unmoving, not sure if she should speak.

"Consistently," he added. He returned to the brittle pages, reviewed some details and again fixed a stern expression on Grace, "You swear too much."

"Are those infractions really big enough to keep me out of Heaven?" Grace asked.

"Well, there's more."

"Excuse me, sir, but if we're where I think, we just want to see our mom. Her name's Debra?" Holly said.

"Our names change with each life. Once she's-- hold on, Debra? Debra?" he said, looking back and forth in surprise between their faces. Two handed he closed the oversized tome. "Why didn't you say so? Everyone knows Debra."

The sisters' excitement became instantly palpable.

"She lets people pick the lavender that grows in her front yard. What a generous soul. Always hanging out with her kids. Such a sweet lady."

Their faces dropped.

"What do you mean, hanging out with her kids? We're her kids," Grace said.

"I mean all her other kids."

"Other kids?"

The gates parted and clouds on either side swirled dramatically in response to the momentum.

"Thank you," Holly said and grabbed her sister's arm to rush in before there was any second guessing.

    He called after them, "Go on in and pick some lavender for me. It's always the best."

3

Purple airy mounds covered the entire front yard. A sign on the white picket fence read: FEEL FREE TO PICK THE LAVENDER. NO NEED TO ASK. The house had a glow. Everything gave off a certain radiance.

Grace clicked open the low latch on the other side of the gate. On the short distance to the front porch the purple tufts brushed against them, releasing a piney floral fragrance. Holly knocked and a man with linebacker shoulders and a blond bowl haircut opened the door.

"You can go ahead and pick the lavender. No need to ask," he said and stepped back to shut the door. Grace shot her hand out to stop it.

"We're not here for the lavender. We're here for our mom."

"I think you have the wrong house," the man said with a friendly smile.

"Does Debra live here?"

"My mom's Debra. She lives here," he said studying their faces, "Oh yes, I've seen you at the

Windows. If she's your mom and she's my mom that makes you my sisters."

He reached out and embraced the two together at once. Grace and Holly each put their outside hands on his back. Where the two stood shoulder to shoulder, their arms hung limp and useless.

The fresh green plush carpeting matched the green sofa, love seat and upholstered chairs. Coordinating wallpaper of green winged parrots on broad banana plant leaves wrapped around the living room. Two carpeted steps and a small metal railing lead to the sunken room.

"Everyone come on down. We have new sisters," the blond bowl cut man called upstairs. Three women spilled down a stairway closely followed by a little girl dolled up in a ruffle dress with a white pinafore.

The exuberance was overwhelming. Grace and Holly chocked this up to Heaven. The three women, all with waist length light brown hair and long dresses that brought to mind frontier life, came bursting with exclamations and questions.

"We have new sisters!"
"Hot dog!"
"What joy!"
"When did you get here?"
"What else have you seen?"

"Have a seat."

"Oh, do have a seat."

The instant Grace sat on the green velvet sofa the small dark haired child, who appeared no older than a kindergartener, hopped up on her lap and made herself comfortable.

"I'm Grace. What's your name?" the little girl said.

"*I'm* Grace," Grace said.

"We match," the child said in a dreamy little voice and wrapped her arms around Grace's neck, the weight forcing her to hunch her back.

"You'll live here with us."

"We'll have to get a bigger dinner table."

"We can fit. It's only two more chairs."

"We love the dinner table, sitting in a circle. Sometimes we just hold hands and sing."

With the child still attached to Grace, and the pull and the strain, something snapped.

"We have the wrong house," Grace announced, extricated herself from the young girl's arms and stood to go.

"What are you doing? This is your home now too," the man said shaking his silky blond hair out of his eyes.

"You're so generous. This has all been a bit much and we're..." Grace searched for the words as she worked her way to the door, "...We're really the only kids our mom ever had. It was just us. We must have the wrong house."

Holly, close behind, added, "Our mother passed when we were young. It's been about twenty years, so right now, all we want to do is see her again. We'll come back and chat later." Grace pulled the front door as someone on the other side pushed. The second it opened, Holly breathed out, "Oh, it's you," and fell into her mother's arms.

"Girls! Girls! This is a huge surprise," Mom said. "I hope nothing bad happened. Well, that doesn't matter. We're all here. All together again."

Mom held onto Holly tight with one arm and extended her other wide to collect Grace. Before Grace could move forward of her own accord she felt herself being thrust from behind as Mom's other adult children closed in for a group hug. Sandwiched in the folds of the familial cluster, Grace forgot everything else while she clung to her mother and sister. That long hoped for, unattainable dream, suddenly real.

Eventually, the crowd released their hold and the embrace loosened.

"These people are your kids?" Grace asked

"I guess over the course of my lives I've had a few," Mom laughed, "Meet: Ansel, Tammy, Mary,

Bertha Begonia and then the little one is Grace."

"I'm Grace," Grace said placing her fingertips to her chest.

"I know. Isn't that funny? I guess I must have liked the name so much I used it a couple times. We lost her young," Mom said with a touch of the solemn, distantly remembering, "But now she's forever the baby of the family. Isn't that so?" She crouched down and the two touched noses. "Come along girls. We're going to be late."

"Late for what?" Holly asked.

"Craft class."

4

    Colorful construction paper awaited them inside the entrance. They each selected a few sheets and headed over to one of the long, smooth, peach-lacquer-top tables. The benches on either side could seat four apiece. Little Grace took up half the space of an adult and Ansel, with his broad shoulders, occupied a space and a half, so it made sense for them to sit on either side of Mom, evening each other out. Tammy, Mary and Bertha Begonia sat together across from them. Grace and Holly found room at the ends of the peachy colored benches, facing each other. Holly and Ansel exchanged a smile as she took a seat next to him.

    All three of Mom's adult daughters: Tammy, Mary and Bertha Begonia were hard to tell apart and seemed to be more of a trio than individuals. They looked similar, dressed alike and had long, frizzy, light brown hair that it appeared they brushed, but did nothing else with, as if there were no styling products or hair ties available in the afterlife.

As soon as they all took their seats, people in white robes came with shallow rectangular trays of different pastas sectioned off. They slid three trays in a row down the center of the table so both sides could easily reach.

Little Grace leaned on the table to tell her new sisters, at the other end, "You can request string if you want to make a macaroni necklace. Just let them know."

"Look," Mom pointed out one compartment of the center tray and put her arm around the small dark haired child, "Novelty pasta. Little dinosaurs."

"I think we should request another tray," Bertha Begonia said. "None of these have any spaghetti for me to break up. I want to make sunbeams."

"So you all like crafts?" Grace asked.

"It's Heaven," Mom said, "They have the very best craft classes here. The very best of everything. In the life I had with you two I always wanted to be an artist." She addressed the other kids, "When you're born to a blue collar community you didn't pursue those things. If you were a woman and single you could have a hobby. When you got married extra funds went to the children. Your husband could blow his money on beer with his friends after work, but women didn't get the same pass."

Ansel turned to Grace and Holly and explained, "We had money in our life with Mom. It's good, she gives us a different perspective on how the less fortunate live."

"There was nothing I loved more than spending time with my family," Mom said. "But there was one more thing I secretly hoped for. One Christmas I didn't want anything under the tree. I asked for an art class. I looked over the local library bulletin and what the community center offered. Some of the arts seemed so daunting: figure drawing, watercolor, still life. And then I saw the listing for crafts. Crafts seemed like the most fun. Thought I'd start with that and see where things went. Your father signed me up. I loved that craft class. I learned macramé. Remember we had that nice hanging plant in the kitchen with it? And there was the small pennant I put in the den? It was about the size of a greeting card?"

"I remember, it was burlap. Had two owls made of glazed pretzels or something," Grace said.

"They both had the same tiny, brown felt triangles on top for ears and dried beans for eyes, but one pretzel I turned the double rounded part up for the face and the other I turned it down, instead of creating them the same. The teacher said that was the mark of a true artist, making artistic decisions."

A woman in white robes walked by and Mom flagged her down, "Excuse me, could we please get some spaghetti? My daughter would like to make sunbeams."

"Of course," the passing woman said in a gentle voice.

"I was so proud of that owl banner and none of you missed an opportunity to make fun of it. I asked for the class because..." Mom got sheepish, "...I thought someday I'd, maybe, if I really tried, I could do art like Michelangelo or Georgia O'Keeffe or something. I looked at my owls with their little pretzel faces and realized I was dreaming. I took it down and the jokes stopped and I didn't ask for anymore classes."

She paused as the tray with spaghetti arrived and slid between them. It shifted the three other trays down the center line.

"When I got here they told me you've arrived. Your dreams can come true. I immediately started studying to be like one of the great artistic masters. The training was meticulous and serious. That's what I thought I wanted. Then in time I saw what I really wanted, what I really want, is to be with my family all day long and make fun crafts."

"We'd love your owls, Mom. Nobody makes owls like you," Bertha Begonia said while gluing her spaghetti sunbeams in place.

"You kids are the best." Mom looked down the table at the new girls, "You girls are the best too. You're all the best!"

"I'm sorry we made fun of it," Grace said, "I'm so, so sorry."

"It's already forgotten. You girls were so young I don't blame you in the slightest. You were just following your father's lead."

"What happened after that, Mom?" Ansel asked.

"Well, I went back to being a housewife and eventually the cancer came and took me. That's how it goes... But here we're all together. Look at us. Things couldn't be better."

Over the center trays, Holly slid her pink sheet of construction paper toward Mom.

"Let's see what you're doing there," Mom said.

"I laid rigatoni zig zag, like tiles," Holly said, "I thought instead of using different pastas to create a picture of something else, the repetition could be the focus. But I don't really know what I'm doing."

Mom held it up off the table, "Yes, the

texture and pattern of the rigatoni, it creates movement, I think. Look at that. You're a natural."

"Look Mom, Grace is doing something very avant-garde," Tammy said and turned back to Grace, "You're into abstract art?"

"I just haven't done this in a long while," Grace said touching her sticky middle finger and thumb together, then parting them again and again. "I guess I'm not really feeling inspired."

"Are you not feeling inspired, or are you afraid to try?" Tammy gave her a cute side eye as if to say I'm on to you. Grace stopped with the sticky fingers. "I know it's something new and can be intimidating, but if you really try, you might surprise yourself."

"Thank you. I'll try," Grace said through a forced grin.

Tammy smiled to herself, happy to impart some encouragement and wisdom to her new sister.

"Class is almost over. They're coming around," Ansel said.

A pleasant woman in white robes leaned down slightly from the waist and asked Grace, "Would you like to hang it on the display wall, take it with you or throw it in the trash and start over next time?"

"Can I just leave it here? I don't want to

walk around Heaven with my macaroni art."

"Let's go to the Windows," Mary suggested.

Mom agreed, "Yes, let's show you the Windows."

5

A cloudless sky above radiated the richest blue that seemed if it were to fall on them they could swim in it. The birds sang in the trees and everyone's lawns grew lush.

The walking formation started as a gathering around Mom. Eventually working its way into Mom flanked by one of her kids on either side, everyone else trailing behind, Little Grace at the very back.

"I'm gonna get lost with all your new kids," Little Grace called.

"Come here," Mom said. The child worked her way through all of Mom's adult children to the front. Mom picked her up and carried her, the child's ruffle pinafore getting bunched up in the mix.

A lady approached, "Debra, I'm creating a lavender wreath thanks to you."

"You'll have to let me see it when you're done. Francesca, these are my other girls. They just arrived. Grace and Holly."

"Isn't your little one Grace?"

"I know, I must have liked the name so much I reused it."

"Haven't seen you both in a while," another woman said, joining the conversation.

"Samantha, these are my other daughters: Grace and Holly."

"Isn't the youngest Grace? The name so nice you used it twice?"

"We were just joking about that," Mom said with a chuckle.

Amidst the jocularity Grace gestured for Holly to step away with her. They casually meandered a few paces back.

"Mom seems pretty popular here," Grace said.

"We had to drop her name to get in the gates."

"Is this what you thought it would be?"

Holly shook her head, "As stupid as it sounds, I thought she'd say 'This whole time I've been waiting for you.' She'd be crying. We'd run to her and she'd spread her arms wide, but..." Holly could only see the top of Mom's head amidst the crowd. "...It appears she's been occupied."

"This entourage is sucking all our Mom time," Grace said.

"That's what everyone says when there's other siblings. She's just giving equal attention."

"But we're new here."

"Maybe she feels it's eternity so we have forever to catch up? No rush?" Holly suggested with a questioning shrug. "Her death created a vacuum in our lives. Maybe for her, when she got here, all voids were filled, family to be with and nothing but fun. She has a new life and we're just showing up."

"At least craft class is done," Grace said.

"Something to be said for small blessings."

"Maybe in the future we could bail on craft class."

"That may be the only way to see Mom. I'm not sure we should be taking invites for granted."

"You're doing better at it than I am."

"Am I?"

"You and Mom both appreciate the artistic medium of rigatoni."

"I don't care about rigatoni," Holly whisper-barked. She looked over at the group to make sure they didn't hear. "I just want to be part of the gang. When it comes to hanging with Mom, I get the feeling we're not cool enough." A bout of laughter erupted from the group. One of the women said Debra you're so funny. "This is eternity. Let's try to fit in otherwise, I don't know what the alternative will be. Who will we do things with? Where will we stay? Who'll look out for us? I don't know how this place works."

They glanced over to see Mom, the obvious bright spot at the center, all her other kids and neighbors orbiting and hovering.

"I think we should make the best of it," Holly added, adjusting her ponytail.

Grace shook her head angry, "I wish we could just get rid of those kids."

"Get rid of them? In Heaven? I don't know. I don't know that that's really the vibe of the place."

"Girls, are you coming?" Mom called over.

In unison, "Yes."

6

Black fabric hung in all the entryways that lined the dove gray hallways. Mom pulled back a weighty portiere and the three of them piled into a small lightless black room.

A waist high Window at the center pitched down at an angle. Holly rested her fingertips on the frame as she peered into it. Mom secured the black cloth flush to the doorframe and a scene rose up, casting a dull glow on their faces.

A dreary sky and long-needled pine trees came into view. A young girl, fair haired, five or six-years-old like Little Grace, lined up stuffed animals and a doll by a front stoop. The pine needle thatched ground made a dry sound underfoot as she situated her audience.

The girl reordered her toys for quite a time: the bear, the bunny, the plastic doll with the stretched out arms that could twist at the hip and shoulder joints, the gray elephant with the loose left eye. Then switching the bunny, the bear and so on.

Nothing much happened so eventually Grace asked, "What are we looking at?"

"Grandma Tina," Mom said. Both Grace and Holly leaned forward, the light getting brighter on their faces.

"What? Where is she?" Holly asked.

"She lives in the hills in a cabin."

"Why is her face all dirty?" Grace asked.

"Her mother's a prostitute so she's not really cared for."

"She looks gaunt."

"There's often not enough food."

"Is this really her life now? How could this happen to Grandma?"

"When a soul is born it's a roll of the dice. Lots of people have children. Whores have children. Those children have souls too."

Grandma shifted her ill-fitting simple dress. The ends of her fair, chin length hair stuck together as if she'd gone swimming and the tips just grazed the water's surface. But it wasn't wet clumping her hair; it was grime.

"With a start like that, what does life have in store for her?" Holly asked, distress working its way into her voice.

"You only get so many chances in life. Some get more than others." Mom leaned closer, peering down, to get a better view, "Some don't get their fair share."

Grandma Tina stopped rearranging and put her palms facing out flat, like now we're all set.

"She has a few opportunities down the line, but more than likely she'll get into the family business young," Mom added.

"Can we help her?"

"We can't help her here. We can only watch."

"What if we went back?"

"If you choose to go back, the chances of your paths crossing in the next life are slim. Even if you did somehow meet, she'd be no one to you. She'd just be somebody's filthy child."

"She had a hard life when we knew her," Grace said, "Dammit. Did Grandma ever have it good?"

"No, not once, but she keeps trying. God love her."

Little Grandma Tina started singing a song, it seemed she made up as she went along as there was no refrain, of dreams coming true and love finding a way.

"You want to watch the people you care about, but honestly, life is kind of boring," Mom said. "Either way, it doesn't matter. You can't hold on to anything from your old life."

Mom pulled back the black fabric and the

images disappeared before their eyes, the light from the hallway replacing the light from the Window.

Grace and Holly reluctantly left. In the gray hallway Mom put a hand on each of their shoulders and smiled warmly from one to the other, happy that they got to do that together.

"Oh, hello," Grace said.

"Hello," a man in white robes pressed his chest to her arm and shoulder as he held her in a nice side bear hug. With a serene grin he explained, "Seems like someone needs a hug." Their faces inches away, Grace turned her's slowly to her mother with an air of curiosity. Should she be alarmed or go with the flow?

Mom's demeanor shifted, her voice became even more pleasant as if in performance for the unannounced guest, "Sweetheart, you're not allowed to swear. I mean, you can. You can do anything you want here but, you know, there are consequences."

"What did I say?"

"D-A-M-- it doesn't matter now, but you used a word that's a no-no."

The Hugger nodded in agreement. Grace remained quite still with the white robed man's arms firmly wrapped around her.

"Mom, we didn't know where you went,"

Ansel said. Mom's other kids followed from around the corner.

"This is Heaven," Little Grace said, pointing to her new sister, "You're supposed to be happy, not a potty-mouth."

Grace glared down at her, the man still attached looked on dotingly, providing the comfort he felt she needed.

"I already told her and it's not your job to scold her," Mom said. Little Grace put her fists to her eyes and began to whimper. The act worked for Mom. "Don't be sad. Come here." And Little Grace ran to Mom, who squatted down to pick her up, and cooed, "There, there, all better."

"Let's go see Uncle Stefan," Ansel said.

Dread washed across Grace and Holly's features at the prospect of viewing another Window. Tammy couldn't help but notice.

"Life is only a series of experiences," Tammy said in her kind, knowing way, "There's no reason to qualify any of it, good or bad. It's all but a blip in time. Don't let what happens in a blip, yours or anyone else's, bother you."

"Tammy's right," Ansel joined in, "Here, in eternity, everything is good. Why worry about anything else? Now come on, let's go see Uncle Stefan."

Ansel led the way. Everyone trailed close

behind. The Hugger followed, hugging Grace, walking foot over foot sideways.

In a new black walled, black ceilinged room, all nine of them crowded around the Window: Mom, Ansel, Little Grace, Tammy, Mary, Bertha Begonia, Holly, Grace and Grace's Hugger. A long slim rectangle of hallway-light edged the portiere, where the fabric fell just shy of touching the doorframe.

"The Window won't run with the curtain open," Ansel said. They jostled about in the darkness, trying to condense themselves to no avail. "There's just not enough room. It's one person too many." Everyone's eyes subtly gravitated to the Hugger. Grace, realizing they two were now a package deal, volunteered to wait outside.

The roars of laughter came in waves with small whispered comments in between. Grace slid her fingers around the edge of the black fabric for a quick peek. The Window went dark and everyone turned to her. She snapped her hand back just as quick, and continued waiting outside in the gray hallway with her companion.

The white robed Hugger finally asked, "Are you feeling better now?"

"Yes, thank you," she said looking straight ahead, drawing out the 's' of yes without meaning to.

"Good."

When he let go Grace pulled the black cloth back to dart in, just as everyone spilled out.

"We watched Ansel's Uncle," Holly said, "He told jokes on his yacht. They were pretty funny."

"Yeah, I could hear. I mean, I could hear the laughter."

"You've seen some Windows. Let's show you the Tunnels," Mary said.

7

"And here are the Tunnels," Mom said, "After the Windows, if you feel adventurous, you can jump right back in, give it another go." A series of perfectly circular openings, the size of hula hoops, lined the hallway.

"Jump back into life? This is the most crazy-ass thing I've ever seen," Grace said, mostly to herself.

"They used to be gray like the walls, but recently they painted the interiors of the Tunnels pink. Seems more appropriate. Don't you think?"

"Lacks subtlety," Grace said, "Should have gone with aqua blue. They already look like tubes in a water park."

"Especially with the signs above," Holly added.

Above each Tunnel a mounted square sign decreed: ONLY ONE AT A TIME.

Grace and Holly inched closer to an opening. The soft hollow sounds of wind originating far off ricocheted and echoed.

"How do you know if you'll see those you love again? Your friends? Your family?" Holly asked.

"What about people you don't even think of? Like the ones who catch you up to speed on the good TV at work?" Grace said.

"All will be reunited here someday. But you jump in a Tunnel it's anyone's game. It's a big world. If you're lucky you go to a developed nation. Clean water," Mom said, narrowing her eyes with a nod to say you know what I mean. Mom stretched her neck and shoulders up to survey the steep slope of the Tunnel, happy to see from where she stood, "Like I said before, most likely these people you knew, you won't cross paths with them again in life. Even if so, who knows if you'll recognize each other? When you return you can't take anything with you. You've got to let go."

With that empty reassurance, Grace and Holly bent at the waist and peered down. Their heads and bodies blocked the light from behind. A few feet in front it was too dark to see, and still that low, lonely howl rose up.

"Why are there so many Windows and so few Tunnels?"

"Oh, there's never a line for the Tunnels. It takes courage to be born," Mom said.

"I don't think I was giving you a good enough hug," the Hugger reappeared and held Grace tight, resting his head on her shoulder. His hair itched her neck and cheek.

Mom greeted the Hugger, "Hello again."
"Hello."

"Do you two know each other?" Grace asked.

"No, but we all adore each other here," Mom said and leaned in to Grace's free ear, "Sweetheart, listen, no swearing. Absolutely no blasphemy. Just do what you can..." she inhaled sharply, gave a broad smile to the Hugger which he gave back. She again came closer to her daughter to whisper, "Try your best. Don't summon the Huggers."

"We're gonna be late for craft class," Bertha Begonia said flipping her excessively long, subtly frizzy hair over her shoulder.

"We just got back from craft class," Grace said.

"That was 'macaroni art'. Now it's 'fun with yarn'."

8

The grand looms came through first. Yarn carts followed. People in white robes wheeled everything out: the yarn by the door and the projects-in-progress to the far end of the opposite corner.

Mom and her adult kids made their way to their grand looms, the weaving already started, they just had to pick up where they left off.

Once Grace and Holly selected some colorful balls and pre-spooled wands, a woman in white robes led them to a table, near the door, where children sat.

"Can't we use yarn over there? We really want to just do stuff with our mom," Grace said.

"Patience, you're not there yet," the woman explained in a gentle voice. The children at the kid's table shifted down on the benches to make room. Little Grace patted the spot next to her for Holly. Grace sat across from them, facing the wall.

"So since you're both new, first off, welcome. Second, I'm going to stand by and coach you to help everything come together."

"Why is mine so small?" Holly asked, looking past Grace at the sizable frames the adults worked on at the far end of the room.

"Ours aren't even looms. They're squares with pegs along the edge," Grace said.

"You're right. Good eye, they're actually not looms. They're called pegboards," the woman in white robes said.

"We use them at the kid's table," Little Grace said.

"We're not even gonna make anything anyway. Can't we get an actual loom near our mom?" Grace asked, turning around to look at the others.

"You're still beginners. So when you're done you'll have a pot holder, or if you make two you can stitch them together and have a tea cozy. Then you can graduate to a bigger loom and make a scarf, or if you stitch a few together, a poncho."

Grace held her tongue on the necessity of a poncho in her new life in Heaven. The girls started winding yarn around the pegboards. Little Grace didn't need guidance. She'd done this before.

"So this is craft day? We hit all the classes?" Holly called over to Mom.

"We all love crafts. This is every day," Mom called back.

"Everyday?"

"Don't worry, there'll be more later," Bertha Begonia said, "'Understanding your glues', 'colored pencils', 'clay pottery', 'advanced construction paper', 'glitter accents'."

"What? What'd she say? I couldn't hear," Grace said. The spacious room that could accommodate hundreds did not lend itself to ideal acoustics.

"Weave the yarn through gently," the instructor said.

"That's what I'm shooting for," Grace said.

"See the bunching and sticking out? Smoothly integrate."

From the opposite corner of the room Mary said, "Mom, tell them the joke you made last time that had us all in stitches."

"Which one?" Mom asked.

"Remember, we were in 'understanding your glues' and you made that joke about mucilage?"

Grace looked over her shoulder and back to Holly, "I can't hear." The woman in white tapped the pegboard to bring her attention back.

"How did it start?" Mom thought aloud for a moment, "Mary, you remember. You tell it."

"Oh, you tell it best," Mary said

"Well, we were... or was it... oh, it was

funnier the first time," Mom said and waved it off laughing at herself.

"Mom, you're so funny," Ansel said.

Mom's other kids chuckled. Holly joined in the laughter too. Grace looked to her questioning what's funny. Holly shrugged and muttered something about not being able to hear either.

The woman in white robes reached to take Grace's project from her, "Maybe we should start anew. This isn't working out." Grace threw her tiny hand loom on the table, knocking a peg loose that bounced on the ground.

"What the hell is this?" Grace demanded. Everyone in the whole of craft class stopped and looked. Grace swung her legs around to the front of the bench and got to her feet. "You were my mom. Dad didn't bother to be a parent after you died. He figured we'd be fine on our own while he took an extra helping of booze and TV and hanging out at the bar with his friends." She heard her sister push out from the table and come around to stand beside her. Tremors began to overtake Grace's hands. "We dreamed of the day we'd see you. We've been waiting our whole lives to see you again. You were our Mom. When we finally got here you were supposed to be *our* Mom. Who the hell are all these kids?!" From the side, Grace felt Holly put a hand on her shoulder, but it didn't matter. She'd already lost all self-control. The entirety of 'fun with yarn' held their breath.

Mom stepped out from behind her grand loom. Her tapestry of turquoise and lime strung taught behind her.

"Oh Gracie, my little sweetheart. Don't be sad. Come here," Mom said. Mom raised her arms, stretching them out wide. Grace instantly regretted her outburst, realizing this was all she really wanted. Grace spread her arms too and took a step forward towards her mother, just as Little Grace raced past her. Mom squatted down and scooped the child up in her arms, holding her close. "There, there," Mom said, "All better." Everyone looked to Grace, arms out, immobilized like a dancer without a partner. A pillar of salt. Still cradling the child, Mom noticed all eyes on her. When she saw the look on Grace's face, Mom said, "What? She was sad too."

From the side, Grace felt tender arms wrap around her. She turned to see who had reached out in her moment of need.

"Sounds like someone needed a hug," the Hugger said.

9

Grace and Holly sat together on a log, scooped out for sitting, under a large leafy tree. The green above dappled the light. Wildflower fields stretched far before them and further still, in the distance, a mountain range of darkest blue jutted to the sky. Strong gusts at the tops blew snow caps in horizontal sweeps, streaking white.

They watched it as they would a fish tank with everything and nothing going through their minds. Grace rested, aggravated and exhausted. Holly sat in moral support.

Eventually, Grace spoke, "The mountains really are quite lovely."

"They are lovely. Lovely and soothing," Holly said.

"Soothing, yes, soothing."

"Do you feel better?"

"I do."

Holly leaned over her sister and said, "She feels better."

"I don't know that she does," the Hugger

replied, his arms still tightly wrapped around Grace as all three sat together on the log carved for sitting, the long white sleeves of his robe pooling in her lap.

"I sure do," Grace said trying to sound calm and convincing, but unable to get the full snip out of her voice.

"You do?"

Grace nodded, staring forward.

"Well, good. I'm glad I could help," the Hugger said.

Both girls waited for him to take the long walk down the path and out of sight. Once gone, they relaxed their posture.

"I'm sorry. I'm sorry. I'm..." Grace shook her head back and forth trying to find the words, "...sorry"

"Don't be."

"In the middle of my rant when I felt your hand on my shoulder I knew it wasn't just me. I was embarrassing you too. It's one thing to embarrass myself. It's another to drag you down with me."

Holly shifted around in her seat, dumfounded that her sister had misinterpreted her completely.

Holly spoke in a measured way to make sure she was abundantly clear, "I wasn't trying to tell you you were embarrassing me. I put my hand on your shoulder to let you know you weren't alone." Grace glanced up at her sister, touched. "I can't believe how we're being treated. You were just the one to say something. While we were waiting here, with the Hugger," Grace glanced down the path he'd left on as Holly continued, "I've come to two decisions. One, we have to remove all swearing from our vocabulary forever."

Grace slouched forward lacing her fingers together over her knees, "I agree."

"And two, I've had a change of heart about a lot of things, including Mom," Holly said, tightening her ponytail, "She's not even our Mom anymore. She's theirs."

"Yeah, seems that way." Grace slumped down further, dipping her forehead to touch her balled up hands.

"All the same," Holly said, lowering her voice and leaning forward so she could look her sister in the eye, "Let's get rid of those kids."

10

"You mean without Mom?" Bertha Begonia said.

"I've spent lifetimes with each of you. You all should take some time and get to know each other. Good idea, Grace," Mom said.

Grace felt a swelling in her heart, both guilt and joy. She didn't realize how hungry she was for maternal approval until she got it. The last thing she wanted was to cause her mother any distress. Regardless, at this point, Mom's other kids were ruining everything and so it was decided.

At the Windows the others wanted to check in on someone particular, so Grace and Holly hung back. After swaying once, the heavy black fabric fell into place, separating them.

"What's the plan?" Holly whispered.

"We're gonna go to the Tunnels and shove them in."

"That's the plan?"

"*Shh.*"

"That's *a* plan?"

"Do you have a better one?"

"What if Mom finds out?"

"She won't. Plus, we're not doing anything wrong. We're only sending them to life," Grace said.

"I don't know that I'd wish life on my worst enemy. Remember Grandma Tina? It can be so awful there."

"Would you wish Heaven on your worst enemy?"

"It's still Heaven. It's still better than down there."

Grace leaned her back on the light gray wall and shook her head, "You always do this. You say you're in and then bail at the last minute. It's up to you. I'll go with whatever you want. But you need to decide."

They stood in silence in the hallway. From behind the black portiere they heard their siblings erupt into great laughter. The unbridled amusement boomed up loud and before it died down, Holly realized she'd thought all the thoughts she needed to.

"Who do we shove first?" Holly asked.

"Ansel. We'll have to do it together. He's much stronger than us. Then the three grown daughters. Little Grace last."

Holly nodded not seeing any other way.

At the Tunnels Grace said, "I wonder if they're connected. I'll hallo in one and you each stand at an opening and tell me..." Her voice caught in her throat.

Without any prompting, Ansel bent down and dipped his head and shoulders into a Tunnel, "Never really looked before. Sure is dark in here."

Things had taken a turn toward the opportune—but they weren't ready.

Grace stood fifteen paces away. One step away, Holly. The other daughters chattered away, oblivious. But Grace and Holly didn't hear any of their talk. They only heard one noise, that hollow air flow, that sound drawing up from the base, indicating where things needed to go, beckoning.

They were supposed to do it together. If Grace ran over it would alarm him. If she walked normal he'd probably be upright by the time she arrived. Ansel was still a lot bigger and stronger than the two of them, never mind Holly alone.

His back faced them. His body leaned, already partially in. Gravity tugged at his blond Dutch boy hair. Although not perfect, this was a chance, and they knew too well when it came to chances, not everyone got their fair share.

Seconds turned to microseconds like how a fly sees things in slow motion. Holly, who often waited for her older sister's lead, took a deep breathe, stepped forward and pushed.

Down went Ansel. Then—chaos. The plan soured fast. The screams, the struggle that followed happened, it seemed, instantaneously. Bertha Begonia latched each of her hands onto Holly's wrists. Holly danced a distressed robot to try and break away from her clutches. Tammy dashed behind Holly and pinned her arms down. Mary closed her eyes and doggy-paddle-slapped both the air and Grace in equal measures. Little Grace wailed without tears to the ceiling.

Grace rushed to her sister and threw her forearms up, trying to fend off Mary's indiscriminant slapping. In the commotion, Grace couldn't see the child, but her cries acted as a locator. Grace worked her way over and with a duck and swift shove, down the Tunnel Little Grace went, lace pinafore and all.

Clad in white, like one of Heaven's orderlies, a Hugger charged toward Holly, "You need much more than a hug." He grabbed her hard and fast causing her legs to fly out from under her. Holly kicked and twisted in a desperate attempt to free herself, as the Hugger began dragging her away.

"Run, Grace! I hope I see you again someday," Holly cried.

Grace couldn't let her sister get hauled off like that. They were in this together. After booting the little girl, Grace knew it wouldn't be long before a Hugger came for her. She had to act fast. She reached for the only thing within grasp, the square sign above a Tunnel. Grace stepped on the lower lip on the circular opening, balancing her feet to get leverage and ripped the sign from the wall. Taking wide broad strokes, she whacked everyone in her way: Tammy, Mary, Bertha Begonia, and finally the Hugger affixed to Holly like a parasite.

"This is Heaven!" the Hugger cried, "What are you doing?!"

Grace swung the sign overhead pummeling down on his shoulders, his back, until the Hugger loosened his grip in pain. Grace yanked Holly away by her clothing, getting her sister to her feet. She braced herself with a hand on the wall so they wouldn't fall into the Tunnel's dark mouth inches away.

Stomping footsteps announced another Hugger's arrival. He marched toward them from behind, more seething than the first. Surrounded, with the angry trio and a Hugger at either end of the hallway, Grace grabbed hold of her sister's hand as they, out of options, looked down into the darkness and jumped.

11

"I've done hundreds of caesarians in my career and I've never seen this. Never. Nurse, get the camera," the doctor said.

"What is it?" the mother asked. She jostled her body up from behind the mint colored tent set up around her belly, "Why aren't they crying?"

"We'll suction their mouths shortly. They're in no danger. I want you to see them first. Nurse, camera!"

In the windowless white room, the nurse drew the camera and flashed a blinding light. Before anyone's eyes could adjust she flashed once more.

The doctor brought them around to show the mother, "They must have developed in the same amniotic sac."

No one uttered a word.

The doctor, the attendants and nurse all cast their gaze in wonder. The mother covered her mouth and began to softly weep. The father beside her rose from his stool, awestruck. Soon the nurse would clean out their nostrils and mouths that would bring on the cries and their first breaths in this world.

In the beautiful silence the doctor said, "You have two girls. They were born holding hands."

My YA novel KUDZU is available at your local bookstore or online.

Feel free to follow me on Instagram: @stacey.osbeck

Made in the USA
Middletown, DE
09 December 2020